Con Men

by

Catherine Johnson

Illustrated by Kevin Hopgood

To anyone who's ever been conned –
may you never be fooled again!

You do not need to read this page –
just get on with the book!

First published in 2009 in Great Britain by
Barrington Stoke Ltd
18 Walker St, Edinburgh, EH3 7LP

www.barringtonstoke.co.uk

ISBN: 978-1-84299-696-6

Printed in Great Britain by Bell & Bain Ltd

Contents

Chapter 1
Can You Tell a Lie?

Can you look your best mate, your mum, in the eye and tell her what she wants to hear without cracking a hint of a smile? Can you do it without flushing pink, without looking away or letting your voice wobble, even a bit?

If you can do all that, you may have some of the skills of the world's most famous con men. Con men gain your confidence and then they trick you. That is why they are called confidence tricksters.

There are as many names for confidence tricksters as there are ways that they cheat you. You will never have heard of most of them – 'grifters', 'hustlers', 'scammers', 'sky-farmers', 'flat catchers', 'illywhackers' ...

All over the world con men have found ways of getting money out of people – and not just fools or the greedy. Con is short for confidence and confidence is another word for trust. These men are criminals. They gain the trust of the public in order to trick them into handing over their money. The tricks and scams they work are known as confidence tricks. Criminals who gain the confidence of the public in this way are known as confidence men, or con men.

Con men and women have been around for as long as history. Stories about them are popular in every country across the world. People have always loved tales where a hero's clever tricks get him a better life, or just out of some fix he is in. We love to see the greedy baddie lose out to a clever, skilful trickster. Heroes like this, from Puss in Boots, who tricks his way into a fortune for his master, to those in modern Hollywood films, are as popular as ever.

However, most small-time con men also spend their time tricking weak and lonely people out of money too. These are the sort of con men you might meet on any street in Britain. They go round knocking on doors. They carry out small, nasty, little cons that take the savings of plain, honest people.

Con men are thieves who steal money from other people. In stories they may not use force, and often target only the greedy and wealthy, those who seem to deserve it. In real life they go for people who are really hard up or very sad. Lonely or old people, who are so pleased to see a kind face and have a chat that they'll hand over their life

savings. These con men are about as far from heroes as you can get.

In this book we'll look at some of the most famous scams and tricks, how they work and how people fall for them – from a gold mine that doesn't exist, to modern Internet scams which are, in fact, new ways of doing old tricks.

So, are your eyes wide open? Are you sure you want to read on? Are you a 'mark' or a 'regular apple'? Do you want to know more about 'grifters' and 'marks', 'Big Stores' and 'cackle bladders'? You do?

Well just remember that writers tell some of the biggest lies around ... how do you know I'm telling the truth or just getting you hooked into reading this book?

Read on and find out!

Chapter 2
A Secret Language

Con men, or 'grifters', as they called themselves, used slang so that ordinary people – called 'apples' – wouldn't know what they were saying. Some of the words first used by grifters over a hundred years ago are still in use, like 'mark' or 'roper', but others in the list below aren't.

MARK: The victim or intended victim of a con.

ROPER or OUTSIDE MAN: The member of the gang who targets the victim and gets him into the con.

INSIDE MAN: The member of the gang who gets most close to the 'mark' and gains his trust. He has to be a brilliant actor and a mind-reader too.

MOB: A con gang.

CACKLE BLADDER: A little rubber bag full of blood – most often from a chicken – used in a fake gun-fight to make it look as if someone has really been shot.

CONVINCER: Cash that the con gang let the 'mark' win or make from a scam before he falls for the final trick.

SHILL: The member of a gang who pretends to be an ordinary person and makes money out of a con.

BLUTE: Fake newspapers or newspaper cuttings used in big con games.

SQUARE PAPER: A really honest person.

TWIST: A female gang member.

WRONG COP: A policeman who cannot be bribed.

RIGHT COP: A policeman who can be bribed!

YELLOW: A fake telegram.

Chapter 3
Everyday Cons

Con men rely on members of the public being so hard up, or so greedy, or so scared and lonely, that they fall for their tricks. But they also charm, trick, and worm their way into the lives of elderly or weak people.

You may have seen people who go around knocking on doors offering to fix roofs. Or they ask if they can do up gardens or put new tarmac on drives. Often there is nothing wrong with the roof, or these con gangs know nothing about gardens or laying tarmac. They are hoping to get paid before they start work, and then they'll be off, without doing anything, taking the money with them!

These con men may look like trades-men. They may have their own van with a mobile phone number painted on the side. They may be charming, and sweet-talk an old person into paying for repairs that aren't even needed. You may think that whoever falls for these scams must be stupid, but the con gangs are all too easy to believe. They make sure that they spend time with their customers, they sweet-talk old ladies and laugh and joke with their 'marks'.

Sometimes the con gangs scare their 'marks' into having work done. They might say that the house is in danger of falling down if the work isn't done. They might seem to be nice and kind but all they care about is getting the 'mark's' money.

These con gangs can see who is going to fall for their sweet-talk and who isn't. And they pick their victims with care. An old person living alone is going to be a far easier target than a husband and wife or a family. A con man will know that it is simpler to charm and to lie to one lonely person than it is to trick a whole family.

Other cons include Internet scams that tell you that you've won a lottery you never even entered – or emails from overseas asking for help in getting huge amounts of money out of war-torn countries. The emails might be sob stories of widows with children who can't get their money from their husbands' Swiss bank accounts. They tell you that they need someone with a British bank account to transfer the money into and they promise you'll get a cut of the millions of pounds that are just waiting to be picked up.

Some Internet scams don't even bother with a letter. They use email. It may look as if it comes from a bank. It says there's a problem with your account and asks you to 'just take a few moments to re-enter your password and account details.' Con men set up fake web sites that look just like the real thing. Once they have got your account details they will take all your money too.

These con men send out thousands of emails in the hope that they will get one reply. And the trick must work because every week there are more!

The most simple of cons is the man or woman who knocks on your door and asks you for a small sum of money. They might tell a story that their child's been hurt and they need to get to the hospital but can't afford the bus fare. Or their electricity meter has been cut off and they just need a

pound coin. Have you had this happen
to you?

It is true that there are some people who
are in real need of money for some good
reason. You have to work out who is telling
the truth and who is lying. You might rely
on the look on their face, the way they tell
the story or the sound of their voice. And it's
still hard to know whether someone is lying
or not. And it's ten times harder when the
only contact you have with them is over the
Internet!

There are also cons where things are
offered for sale that never work. People
spend millions of pounds every year on
slimming pills, cures for baldness or ways to
make you grow taller. Or you might have
seen those signs on lamp posts or that come
through your door – EARN THOUSANDS OF
POUNDS WORKING A FEW HOURS A WEEK IN

YOUR OWN HOME!!!!! If the advert really was true, wouldn't we all be doing it?

The truth is that if anyone offers you something for nothing, watch out! It could be cheap designer clothes, or a way of getting rich quick just by handing over your Paypal account details. But if it really sounds too good to be true, back off. It must be a con!

Chapter 4
The Classic Cons

Confidence scams reached their high point in the 1920s in America. There were many reasons for this. Phones were rare and people used letters, which took a long time to arrive and which could be faked, or telegrams, a basic service which carried messages over a network of wires. Many people didn't understand how this service worked, so con gangs used it to fool them.

But there was another more important reason than the phone lines or the telegram system why these cons worked. America was the top place for people to go who wanted to get rich quick. There was a belief that anyone could make a lot of money in the States. You didn't have to be born into a rich family or have an education. There were stories of people finding gold or oil and making millions very fast, so people were willing to stake all the money they had. They wanted to make a huge fortune as quickly as possible. There were thousands of people landing off the boats every day who hoped that America would be paved with gold.

There would be con men waiting for them as they got off the boats in New York, offering to sell them gold mines or oil fields that didn't in fact exist. If the poor 'marks' were able to travel on across America, they would find out that the pieces of paper sold to them in New York were as much use as toilet paper.

The new towns in the far west – the 'Wild West' – of America were often lawless with little or no police force. Con men set up gambling dens where all the card games were rigged. They promised huge fortunes to anyone foolish or greedy enough to believe them. There was even a con called the Money Box, where a con man would sell a 'mark' a machine that he promised would print real money. Some people were so keen to get rich they would believe it!

And of course if a 'mark' ever tried to find the con man who had taken their money he'd have vanished.

Another important reason con men did so well at this time was the way the American police force worked. Each county or small town ran its own force. So there were plenty

of chances for con men to get local policemen to 'look the other way' for a share of whatever the con mob made out of their unlucky 'mark'. Even in the big cities like New York or Chicago, it was possible for the bigger con mobs to bribe policemen into leaving them alone.

Con men and the top mobs were seen as the kings of the criminal world. They were looked up to as men who 'never had to get their hands dirty'. They were men and women who used craft and cunning, not force, to get the greedy to hand over their money. Their 'marks' were often seen as fair game. Con men used to say "You can't con an honest 'mark'," and it's true. If someone's really honest, they aren't interested in taking part in any kind of scam, even if it seems as if it will make them a small fortune.

And the reason so many cons do work is that most of us like to think that there is an easy way of making money. We like to think that we know something others don't or that we are smarter than other people. We like the idea that we're different. Con men want us to think we are that much more clever. They want us to think that is why we have been chosen to take part in their schemes. We are so clever we can see how easy money can be made where others can't. So we deserve a big win or a pile of money to fall right into our laps. And if we were honest we'd know that you never, ever, get something for nothing!

Chapter 5
The Big Store

This is one of the most famous big cons there is – it's a way con men have used to take millions of pounds from 'marks' over the years and is so famous it has been shown in many great films. Big cons really got going in the early 1900s.

The Big Store is really the name of a whole family of confidence tricks. The first ever Big Store was just that. It looked like a Pound Shop (in America a 'Nickel and Dime

Store'), where nothing costs more than a pound. The windows were full of all sorts of useful things, all at very cheap prices to draw people into the Big Store. However, if you did step inside you'd just find tables with groups of men playing card games such as Find The Lady or Poker. You would see people looking just like you winning piles of cash. Very soon you'd be led over to a table by a smooth talking con man who'd tell you he'd just won five dollars and you should give it a try too – why it was easy money!

If you did sit down at a table you might win a few dollars in the first game, but from then on you'd lose every time. The games were all rigged and the only people who won were the con men who ran the Big Store.

And none of the items in the shop window ever got sold!

In the years before and after World War One the Big Store changed. Some con men had worked out scams that could steal tens of thousands or sometimes millions of dollars from 'marks' at a time. Rather than dodgy card games, a Big Store con relied on an army of con men. They were like actors in a play. There would be a Director, and a large number of extras. It was all worked out to fool rich men and women into handing over their money. The way a classic Big Store con worked was like this ...

Let's think up a plot. A spoilt young man, his name's Arthur Jones, comes fresh off the train in New York City. It's 1920 and the streets are full of cars and trams, even a few horse drawn carts. The trains are raised up on bridges that criss-cross the city. They spit out dust and smoke as they go. The blocks are so tall they blot out the sky – Arthur has never seen anything like it. So many people dashing around, so much noise!

No mobile phones yet, but there are phone boxes on the street corners and telegraph offices if he ever needs to send a message back home. Arthur comes from Buffalo, where his father runs a bank. He wants Arthur to join the family firm, to start as a clerk on a tiny wage, and work his way up to be manager. Arthur is angry. He knows he is worth more than that!

Arthur thinks he'll show his dad something. He'll make his own money. So he's come to New York to make a fortune as fast as possible. He's wearing his very best suit and smart Sunday best hat. Arthur thinks he looks a million dollars.

Arthur studies the street map in his pocket, but it looks confusing. Outside it has started to pour with rain. Arthur sits down in a coffee shop just inside the station, one of the more expensive ones. He's heard that New York is a city full of crooks and he's not

going to risk mixing with riff-raff. Arthur Jones tells himself he's no fool.

Arthur sits down and orders, takes out the map again and puts it away as a waitress brings his coffee. Another man, not much older than Arthur asks if he may sit down.

"Sure," Arthur says.

The man tells Arthur his name – Ken Harper – and his life story and Arthur nods and smiles, but he wishes the guy would shut up. Arthur is sure his suit is more expensive than Ken's and one thing Arthur doesn't want now he's in the city is cheap friends. Ken tells Arthur that he works in an office in New York. Arthur tells him his father owns and manages a bank in Buffalo. That shuts the guy up.

Arthur takes out the map again and gets up to go. He's almost at the door when Ken taps him on the arm.

"Excuse me, sir! You've dropped this!"

Arthur turns round and sees Ken holding a fat black leather wallet. He puts it into Arthur's hand, but Arthur can feel his own wallet safe and snug in his pocket.

"No, sir!" Arthur says. "This isn't mine." Up close Arthur can see it's stuffed with dollar bills. Arthur and Ken look at each other. A million things race through Arthur's head. Why did he say it wasn't his? After all, just think of the things he could do with all that money! Some of the bills look like fifty-dollar notes! Arthur tries not to look too amazed – there's enough cash there to buy a brand new motor car! Arthur gulps. The man is looking back at him and he doesn't want to look like he's some greedy no good.

"We should hand it in – to the police," Arthur says. He's still holding the wallet. He doesn't really want to give it back to Ken.

"Well, maybe there's an address inside," Ken says. "We could hand it back. We may get a reward."

Arthur nods. A reward would be better than nothing, even if he wasn't the person who found the wallet. Maybe he should stick with Ken for now.

They both sit down and order some more coffee and open up the wallet. Apart from the money – more than Arthur has ever seen outside of his father's bank – there's a card with an address and an old newspaper cutting.

"Heck! I've heard of this guy!" Ken says. "He makes fortunes on the horse races. Always wins! Why, he made so much in

Atlantic City they banned him from the race-track!"

Arthur looks at the picture in the newspaper cutting. The name under the picture reads *Mason Glendale*. Arthur has never heard of him but he nods. He doesn't want to look like a fool.

"Let's go to his office right now!" Ken says. "It's not far from the station."

Arthur wishes he was going on his own, but Ken knows the city and he was the one who picked the wallet up.

Arthur is amazed when it turns out to be a hotel. A very expensive hotel with a marble floor in the lobby and smart staff in uniform. They march up to the desk and ask for Mr Mason Glendale.

"Mr Glendale is not taking visitors at present," the man behind the desk says.

"Tell him we know he's lost something," Ken says. "Tell him that."

After a while they are sent up to his rooms.

Mr Glendale opens the door himself. The view of the city through the huge glass windows is jaw dropping. It's not just a hotel room, it's a whole set of rooms. It even has a sitting room. On a table there is a ticker tape machine. Arthur's father doesn't even have one in his bank! It's a state of the art, up to date bit of high tech (in 1920) – and this guy has one right in his room. Arthur tries not to stare.

"You have my wallet!" Mason Glendale says. He's thrilled. He takes a box of cigars and offers them round then pours them all drinks. Why that wallet, he says, belonged to his daddy and *his* daddy before that. Mason Glendale is so grateful he offers to take

Arthur and Ken out for dinner at the most expensive restaurant in New York. It's full of celebrities and Arthur's suit looks a bit shabby.

Arthur sits back in the padded seat of the restaurant and smiles. This is the life he wants. He doesn't want to be tied to some small-town bank – he doesn't want to work hard for thirty years like his father. He wants money now, and lots of it. He wants the high life, and a limo like the one Mr Glendale took them to the restaurant in.

Arthur listens to Mr Glendale and as the evening wears on they have more and more to drink, Mr Glendale is so grateful for getting his wallet back that he offers them both a reward. He tells Arthur and Ken he'll let them in on a deal, one that can't fail. He lowers his voice and leans close – this would be a sure way of making a profit. He'll phone them tomorrow with the name of a horse and

they'll place the bet. He promises it'll win.
Mason Glendale gives them twenty dollars
each reward and says if they put it on that
horse it'll bring them at least twice that.
That's how he makes his own money after all
– and Mason Glendale always wins and never
loses!

Arthur is impressed. "I'd sure like to
know your secret, Mr Glendale," he says.

"Call me Mason! Why you remind me of
my own dear son George," Mason Glendale
smiles sadly. "George died in France in the
war. But no more gloomy thoughts." He calls
over to a waiter. "More champagne!"

If only my dad could see me now, Arthur
thinks.

****

Now of course we know that Mason
Glendale, Ken Harper and nearly all of the

other people Arthur will meet over the next few days are not what they seem. 'Ken Harper' is a skilled 'roper'. He draws in the victim. He watched Arthur get off the train and he saw the swagger in his step. He could tell from the way he walked and looked around that Arthur was vain. He could see from the style and cut of his clothes that the young man had money. Ken could see from the way Arthur acted that he was greedy, that he thought he was better than others. The clincher was finding out that his father ran a bank. As soon as he heard this Ken knew Arthur would be good for a big payout.

'Mason Glendale' is the 'inside man'. His job is to get Arthur's trust and to make him think he's got a sure way of making large amounts of money – with no risk.

The hotel is real – but Mason might have a deal with the manager who gets a cut of the con. Or maybe he's paying him in advance knowing that the money the gang are going to get out of Arthur will pay the costs. And you bet this gang are planning to make sure that Arthur Jones hands over tens of thousands – in post-war America the cons played 'marks' for millions of dollars.

This is a classic Big Store con called The Wire. It works by making the 'mark' – in this case Arthur Jones – think that Mason Glendale has some way of knowing which horse will win. Mason tells Arthur he knows how to tap into the telegraph system (which of course he doesn't). He says that he can delay the results of the races from getting to the gambling clubs (which were like betting shops).

Arthur wants to believe Mason, and why shouldn't he? Mason lives in an expensive hotel and is smooth and charming. Arthur sees the start of a new life. A new world is opening up that he thinks is just right for him.

****

The next day Ken and Arthur are waiting in a coffee shop round the corner from a smart gambling club. The man at the counter picks up the phone.

"Call for Mr Jones!" he shouts.

Arthur tries not to panic. It's Mason. "Put the money on Red Fox to win. Fast as you can!"

Arthur and Ken leave the coffee shop and go to the smart gambling club that Mason has told them about. They tell the doorman they're friends of Mr Glendale and he lets them in. Inside there is a lot going on. One man is writing up results on a board. Another man shouts out the commentary as results come in over the telegraph machine.

There's a cashier and a whole lot of men placing bets. Ken tells Arthur to line up. The race is the 12.15 at Atlantic City and the results are due in ten minutes. In front of him men are placing bets so big Arthur can't believe it. Fifty dollar bets, one hundred dollar bets. These men are waving money around like there's no tomorrow. Arthur takes out the money Mason Glendale gave them.

"Forty dollars on Red Fox to win," he says. The cashier almost laughs at the tiny bet, but puts it into the safe. Arthur can see stacks of money, more than his father's bank in Buffalo takes in a year.

Ken and Arthur sit down. Ken is nervous. The race is about to start and Ken says he could do with twenty dollars. Arthur leans close and whispers, "It's a sure thing, remember!"

The commentator shouts, "They're off!"

Red Fox wins easily. Arthur collects their money – just as Mason has promised. They've won forty dollars each. Arthur and Ken are thrilled, they go back to thank Mason and he promises another horse the next day. Soon twenty dollars has grown into one hundred. Arthur is hooked.

****

At this point you might think the con men have lost money. After all, the gambling club, with its telegraph and cashiers and customers, is all fake and all the men in there, on top of rent of the gambling club, will have to be paid. And the one hundred dollars in Arthur's pocket is real. But it's come from the con men themselves. This money is the 'convincer'. It convinces the 'mark' that there is real money to be made and this is when – if the idea has been

43

planted in the 'mark's' head – the con really begins.

****

Arthur likes this way of making easy money. Ken agrees. "This beats working at the office any day of the week. Just think if we'd put one hundred dollars on a sure thing!"

"One hundred dollars!" Arthur snorts. "Why, there were men in that club betting thousands!"

They go back to Mason at the hotel and thank him. Mason tells them that he is moving on from New York City in a week or so. The police have begun sniffing around – and his methods are, after all, against the law. He says how good it's been to meet them both and he's sorry to go. Ken seems to accept this but Arthur wants to place just

one more bet. He waits until Ken has left.
After all, he doesn't want to have to share a
good idea or any more winnings. Then he
tells Mason his plan. Arthur explains he
could get hold of a large sum from his
father's bank. It would take a few days, but
he could be back in New York at the weekend
and they could place the whole amount and
be rich for life. He'd give the money back
and no one would be any the wiser!

Mason pretends to think about it. Arthur
sees his chance of easy money slipping away.
He decides to go back to Buffalo and come
back with the money before Mason has made
up his mind. Once the money is on the table
there will be no turning back!

****

This part of the con is called 'Putting the
mark on the Send'. By this time the 'mark' is
so keen to make money – even if it is all

illegal – that he will travel hundreds of miles to his home town to get money that he thinks he will be able to double or triple with the 'inside man's' help. Mason doesn't have to ask Arthur to get the money – Arthur wants to. In the past, 'marks' have travelled from Florida to Europe and back again 'On the Send', thinking they will make themselves rich, when all they are doing is bringing the con men money and happily handing it over.

****

Arthur plans to open his father's safe and take every penny, believing he has a chance that's too good to miss. So Arthur sneaks back home. He goes at once to the bank after it has shut on a Friday night. He knows which numbers open the safe. He takes one hundred thousand dollars out and puts it in a bag. His father will never know because he'll return the money before Monday morning.

He gets back on the train for New York, holding the bag tight. He is going to be rich!

The next day, Arthur waits in the café for the phone call. Arthur is nervous. He's carrying the bag with one hundred thousand dollars in it. He drinks his coffee and thinks about what he's going to do with all that money. A trip around the world perhaps? A car? A penthouse apartment? Arthur is nervous and excited. Perhaps the phone won't ring? He bites his nails. His hands shake. At last the call comes.

"Place the money on Fancy Girl in the 12 noon race. I'll be outside the club after the race and we'll split the money." Then that's it, the phone's dead.

Fancy Girl, thinks Arthur as he leaves for the gambling club.

There are people standing in line at the counter, but no one seems to notice and as always there are customers waving huge amounts of cash.

"Fancy Girl," Arthur says.

"To win or evens?" the cashier says.

Arthur feels sick. What did Mason say? Arthur gulps. "To win."

He pushes the money across the counter – not just his father's money, but also the money of all the small farmers and shopkeepers and bank account holders of Buffalo. He has made up his mind that it's worth it to get rich. After all, Mason never loses. Arthur watches as it's put inside the safe.

"They're off!" yells the commentator. Arthur bites his nails. Fancy Girl takes the lead. His heart beats faster and faster as another horse – Lazy Bones – comes up on the inside. It's neck and neck and the result

is a photo finish! Arthur can't believe it, he
tells himself it's only a matter of time and
the result will be that Fancy Girl has won.
Mason Glendale never loses. Arthur goes to
the cashier, who says there's no payout until
the result has been declared. Arthur buys
himself a drink and knocks it back in one. He
is seconds away from his pay out.

Suddenly there's a loud whistle. A police
whistle. The gambling club is full of
policemen. Arthur can't believe it – Mason
Glendale is being marched down the steps
towards him, a policeman holding each arm.
Arthur looks away. He feels very, very sick.

Arthur goes over to the cashier's desk –
he still thinks he can collect his winnings.

"Nobody move!" barks the policeman.

The manager of the club talks in a low
voice to the policeman. Mason flicks a look
at Arthur.

The policeman speaks again. "We are sure there is another man in it with Mr Glendale. And we know he's here!" He points at Mason. The policeman talks to the manager. "Any very large cash bets placed today, sir?" Arthur can feel the blood drain from his face. He doesn't want to go to jail!

Suddenly Mason breaks free from the policeman and pulls a gun. There's a crack and the smell of gunshot, another crack and Mason is on the floor, blood seeping from his mouth. Everyone moves at the same time, the customers run for the street. Arthur can't believe he gets out. Once he hits the street he runs and runs and never looks back.

****

Inside the gambling club, the cons wait until Arthur is out of sight. They lock the front door.

Then, when they are sure Arthur has gone for good, a policeman helps Mason up from the floor and the cons celebrate their hundred thousand dollar pay out. The police were fake, the guns were fake, the blood came from a 'cackle bladder' hidden in Mason's mouth. This fake death will see to it the 'mark' is so scared he won't try and contact the police. This part of the con is called the 'Blow Off'. They want Arthur to be so scared and ashamed that he won't tell anyone what has happened to him.

The con gang strip the gambling club and clear out Mason's hotel room. And if Arthur thinks in a couple of days that the heat has died down and that it is safe to come back and look for the gambling club, it will have vanished along with the money. Arthur has lost everything.

This kind of con has been played for the past hundred years. The Big Store may be a gambling club or a lawyers' office – even an expensive Art Gallery. 'Marks' may be drawn in to bet on stocks and shares, horses, football games, or to buy property or art that doesn't exist.

Whether it's a classic old style con, or a fake trades-man offering to fix your roof, con men will keep on trying to cheat the public. They'll offer you ways to make easy money. They'll tell you what you want to hear. Some of them may even pretend to fall in love with you! Con men will tell any lies they need to in order to get their hands on someone else's hard earned cash. Remember, they will do anything to get their hands on your money.

Con men are always looking for different ways to find victims. They'll use any new idea, the Internet, mobile phones, and I bet by the time I've finished writing this book, con gangs will have come up with a million new ways of getting 'marks' to hand over their cash.

So be careful who you believe, and remember, if anything ever seems too good to be true, then it almost always is.

Barrington Stoke would like to thank all its readers for commenting on the manuscript before publication and in particular:

Susan Dearden
Patina Douglas
James Flower
Catherine Jenkins
Oliver Jones
Ella Mahoney
Cameron McLeod
Shane Adam Paldrey
Liam Petherick
Joseph Pettite
Jamie Pittard
Luke Scriven
Jordan L Smith
Chris Brierley Stamp
William Stradling
Steve Taylor
Christopher Turner

Become a Consultant!

Would you like to give us feedback on our titles before they are published? Contact us at the email address below – we'd love to hear from you!

info@barringtonstoke.co.uk
www.barringtonstoke.co.uk

AUTHOR CHECK LIST

Catherine Johnson

What's the best con you've heard of that you didn't put in the book?

I like the story of Princess Caraboo, who turned up in the West Country over two hundred years ago. She said she was a princess from somewhere in the Indian Ocean, and Bristol society thought she was fantastic. She went to all the dances and was given lovely clothes to wear. It was months before people found out she was really a shoemaker's daughter from Devon.

Have you ever been the victim of a con? If so what was it and what happened?

When I was 13 I went to Petticoat Lane Market and ended up buying blankets that I didn't want from a very hard-talking salesman. I've never been rich enough to be asked to invest in anything. One of my best friends got tricked into a con for *The Real Hustle* and had her shame shown up on the telly for everyone to see!

If you won loads of money at a casino, what would you spend it on?

I'm sure no casino would let me in because I'm too scruffy! I know that gambling is a very easy and exciting way to lose money – I put loads into those penny falls machines in seaside arcades. If I did win loads of cash I'd buy my own horse and have a swimming pool put in the basement.

ILLUSTRATOR CHECK LIST

Kevin Hopgood

Have you ever been the victim of a con? If so what was it and what happened?

I once got an odd e-mail telling me that I'd won $1,000,000.00 in the Nigerian state lottery. All I had to do was to e-mail them my bank details to claim my prize. I knew I had not gone in for any Nigerian state lottery, so I never claimed the prize ...

If you won loads of money at a casino, what would you spend it on?

My wife and children of course! They may be reading this and my life won't be worth living if I don't say I'd spend it on them ...

Which is your favourite con in the book?

I really liked drawing all the cons set in the 1920s. I grew up on a diet of classic old black & white American movies that were on TV all the time in the sixties. At the time I thought it odd that Americans all wore really cool suits and hats while in the UK we were all wearing tank tops and cheese cloth shirts!

Do you think you would make a good con man?

For the past 20 years I've earned all the money I need without having to get a proper job. I'm getting away with it so far!

Time for another Reality Check? Try these!

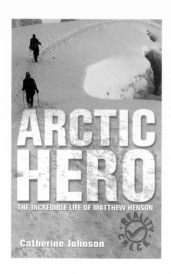

Arctic Hero
by
Catherine Johnson

At the North Pole Matthew Henson battled fear, frostbite and freezing winds. At home in America, he was treated badly – just because he was black. But Matt never gave up ... The amazing adventure of Matthew Henson. Explorer. Survivor. Arctic Hero.

The Day the Island Exploded
by Alexandra Pratt

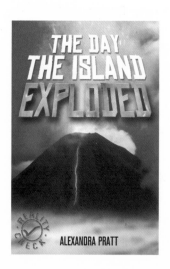

It's the trip of a life-time! Graham's on an island – deep in frozen Antarctica. But one day the ground starts to rumble.
The volcanoes are erupting!
The island is exploding ...
Can he escape in time?

Germ Wars
by
Gill Arbuthnott

The germ that killed 27 million people.
The green fungus that can save lives!
And the 8-year-old boy who became a risky medical experiment ...
Think you know about germs?
Think again!

Snow Tigers
by
Simon Chapman

Snow storms. Forest fires. Armed robbers. Deep in the forests of Siberia, the Captain has to face them all. But in the shadows lurks something much more deadly ... the snow tigers.

You can order these books directly from our website at
www.barringtonstoke.co.uk